Stardust and Wolves

Analesia Brady

BookLeaf Publishing
India | USA | UK

Presentation by *BookLeaf Publishing*

Web: www.bookleafpub.com

E-mail: info@bookleafpub.com

ISBN: 9789363302068

First edition 2024

*To my wolf, my shadow, my best friend that
follows me anywhere - your pawprints will be
on my heart for many life times.*

*To my husband who is the Aragorn to my Arwen
and the Mary to my Pippin - thank you for
pushing me to write and always being down for
an adventure.*

Lovers

He was the waves
And I the rocks
He crashed into my soul
While lovers watched from the docks

Eternity

I like how
Our souls vibe
As if we were lovers
In past lives

Skin Deep

3

He was fresh ink on paper
Leaving stains on my skin
Then I was dismissed
Our story left unfinished

Longing

I want the caress of winter's fire
Your hand
To hold mine tighter

Crave

5

I crave the could be
And what ifs
Love stories
I'll never finish

Fogged

His breath fogged the glass
Much like my heart
Left me in a house of mirrors
Looking for the start

Burn

7

I have always wanted for you
To breathe my name

Now I want to forget
Every way
You stoked the flames

The Sea

8

Maybe if I rest my heart at sea

The tides will let us meet

Midnight

9

My body has learned to crave
Things like you
And the midnight rain

The Heart

My heart is twisted
Tangled in knots
You planted
So many forget me nots

Universes

11

Just another

If it was a different time

Then you would be mine

Dark and Deep

12

My love doesn't stay the same
It flows like the sea
With changing ability
Dark and salty
Much like you
Much like me

Letting Go

13

The way stars fade
I let go of you
In a similar sort of way

Working Man

Broken hearts
Prick a new love's hand

So maybe,
The best lover
Is a soft man
With callused hands

Your Life

15

Magic.
Feeling the butterflies
This is what they mean
By falling in love
With your own life

Seasons

His fingers painted my cheeks
With the blush of Spring
Kisses ignited my soul
like fires lit in Winter
His laughter filled me
Warm like Summer's sun
Best of all,
My heart fell,
Like leaves of Fall

Return To Sender

17

You deserve
Every ounce
Your heart has given

Wild

18

stars shine
wolves sing
people go blind
to love at their feet

Soft

19

there's a softness
I want to keep
I don't want to bury it
at least,
not too deep

Stardust and Storms

People aren't just stardust and light

They are raging fires

Treacherous caverns

Ship wrecking storms

The Moon

21

I wish forgiveness came as easy

As stars forgiving the moon

9 789363 302068